# AI PROMPTS
## FOR CHURCH LEADERS

KATIE ALLRED
& DAVID THORNE, ED.D.

**AI Prompts for Church Leaders**

© 2025 Missional Marketing

All rights reserved.

No part of this publication may be reproduced, stored in a retrieval system, or transmitted in any form or by any means—electronic, mechanical, photocopying, recording, or otherwise—without the publisher's prior written permission, except for brief quotations in reviews or educational use.

**Published by: Missional Marketing**

10115 E. Bell Road

Suite 107, Box 146

Scottsdale, Arizona 85260

Ph: 480.420.2007

info@missionalmarketing.com

www.missionalmarketing.com

**Disclaimer**

This book is designed to provide general guidance and practical AI applications for church leaders. It is not intended to replace theological, legal, or ethical counsel. The authors and publisher disclaim any liability for decisions made based on the contents of this book.

Additionally, this book was created in part using artificial intelligence tools, including **Claude** and **ChatGPT**, to assist in content development and refinement. The authors have reviewed and curated all AI-generated content to ensure accuracy and alignment with the book's intended message.

**ISBN: 978-1-7351960-0-8 Paperback**

**ISBN: 978-1-7351960-1-5 eBook**

**Printed in the United States.**

For bulk purchases, church licensing, or inquiries, contact info@missionalmarketing.com

# Table of Contents

**Introduction** ............................................................................ 1
    *Embracing AI as a Ministry Multiplier*
        Why This Book Matters Now ................................................. 1
        What You'll Discover .............................................................. 2
        Preaching & Teaching ............................................................. 2
        Communications & Engagement .......................................... 3
        Worship Arts ........................................................................... 3
        Pastoral Care ........................................................................... 3
        Discipleship ............................................................................. 3
        Next Gen Ministry .................................................................. 4
        Outreach & Mission ............................................................... 4
        Operations ............................................................................... 4
        How This Book Works ........................................................... 4
        Our Promise to You ................................................................ 5
        How to Use This Book ........................................................... 5
        The Journey Ahead ................................................................. 6

**Chapter 1** ................................................................................. 7
    *AI Essentials for Church Leaders*
        Quick Overview ...................................................................... 7
        Core Concepts ......................................................................... 7
        Prompt Categories .................................................................. 8
        Building Better Prompts ...................................................... 10
        Advanced Techniques .......................................................... 11
        Quick Start Prompts ............................................................. 13
        Practice Workshop ............................................................... 14
        Next Steps ............................................................................. 14

**Chapter 2** ............................................................................... 17
    *AI for Preaching and Teaching*
        Quick Overview .................................................................... 17
        Core Concepts ....................................................................... 17
        Prompt Categories ................................................................ 18
        Advanced Techniques .......................................................... 20
        Time-Saving Strategies ........................................................ 21
        Practice Workshop ............................................................... 22
        Next Steps ............................................................................. 22
        Special SermonSpark Features ........................................... 22

## Chapter 3 .......................................................................................... 25
*AI for Church Communications & Digital Engagement*
    Quick Overview ............................................................................ 25
    Core Concepts .............................................................................. 25
    Prompt Categories ........................................................................ 26
    Advanced Techniques .................................................................. 29
    Time-Saving Strategies ................................................................ 30
    Practice Workshop ...................................................................... 31
    Next Steps .................................................................................... 31

## Chapter 4 .......................................................................................... 33
*AI for Worship Arts & Creative Planning*
    Quick Overview ............................................................................ 33
    Core Concepts .............................................................................. 33
    Prompt Categories ........................................................................ 34
    Advanced Techniques .................................................................. 37
    Time-Saving Strategies ................................................................ 38
    Practice Workshop ...................................................................... 39
    Next Steps .................................................................................... 39

## Chapter 5 .......................................................................................... 41
*AI for Congregational Care & Counseling*
    Quick Overview ............................................................................ 41
    Core Concepts .............................................................................. 41
    Prompt Categories ........................................................................ 42
    Advanced Techniques .................................................................. 45
    Next Steps .................................................................................... 46

## Chapter 6 .......................................................................................... 47
*AI for Discipleship & Small Group Ministry*
    Quick Overview ............................................................................ 47
    Core Concepts .............................................................................. 47
    Prompt Categories ........................................................................ 48
    Advanced Techniques .................................................................. 51
    Time-Saving Tools ........................................................................ 52
    Next Steps .................................................................................... 54

## Chapter 7 .......................................................................................... 55
*AI for Next Gen Ministry: Youth & Children*
    Quick Overview ............................................................................ 55
    Core Concepts .............................................................................. 55
    Prompt Categories ........................................................................ 56
    Advanced Techniques .................................................................. 60
    Next Steps .................................................................................... 62

## Chapter 8 .................................................................................................. 63
*AI for Outreach & Missions Strategies*
- Quick Overview ........................................................................... 63
- Core Concepts ............................................................................. 63
- Prompt Categories ..................................................................... 65
- Advanced Techniques ............................................................... 69
- Next Steps .................................................................................... 70

## Chapter 9 .................................................................................................. 71
*AI for Church Operations & Administration*
- Quick Overview ........................................................................... 71
- Core Concepts ............................................................................. 71
- Prompt Categories ..................................................................... 72
- Advanced Techniques ............................................................... 76
- Next Steps .................................................................................... 77

## Chapter 10 ................................................................................................ 79
*Bringing It All Together - Your Church's AI Journey*
- The Integration Challenge ....................................................... 79
- Understanding Where You Are ............................................... 80
- The Implementation Mountain ............................................... 80
- The Reality Check ....................................................................... 81
- A Better Way Forward ............................................................... 81
- Your Next Step ............................................................................ 83

## Appendix ................................................................................................... 85
*Recommended AI Resources for Church Leaders*
- Essential AI Tools for Ministry ................................................ 85
- Must-Read Books ........................................................................ 86
- Join the Community .................................................................. 87
- Stay Connected ........................................................................... 87
- Ongoing Support ........................................................................ 88
- Looking Forward ......................................................................... 88
- About the AuthorsThe Heart Behind This Book .................. 89

## Meet Your Guides .................................................................................... 91
*Katie Allred, MA*
*David Thorne, Ed.D.*

## The AI for Churches Community ........................................................ 93

## Our Invitation to You .............................................................................. 95

# Introduction

## Embracing AI as a Ministry Multiplier

Imagine walking into your church office tomorrow morning. Your inbox is overflowing. The sermon needs work. Three ministry teams need resources. Social media posts are overdue. And somewhere in the mix, you need to find time for what matters most: connecting with people and sharing God's love.

Now imagine having a dedicated assistant who has read every book on church leadership, mastered every communication platform, and stands ready to help you multiply your ministry impact. This is the promise of artificial intelligence when thoughtfully applied to ministry.

In churches across the globe, this transformation is already happening. Pastors are deepening their sermon preparation through AI-enhanced research. Youth ministers are creating more engaging Bible lessons with AI-generated activities. Worship leaders are crafting meaningful experiences with AI-supported planning. Administrative teams are streamlining operations with AI-powered systems. All of this serves one purpose: freeing up more time and energy for authentic, personal ministry.

## Why This Book Matters Now

The rapid advancement of AI capabilities has created both extraordinary opportunities and unique challenges for church leaders. While some eagerly embrace these new tools, others approach with careful consideration, asking crucial questions:

- How can we use AI while maintaining the authentic, relational heart of ministry?
- What are the practical, day-to-day applications of AI in church work?
- How do we ensure AI serves our mission rather than reshaping it?
- Where do we even begin?

Whether you're tech-savvy or tech-hesitant, this book meets you exactly where you are. We've distilled years of experience in both ministry and technology into clear, actionable guidance for leveraging AI in ways that enhance rather than replace the essential human elements of ministry.

## What You'll Discover

"AI Prompts for Church Leaders" is your practical guide to harnessing AI across every ministry area:

## Preaching & Teaching

- Enhance sermon preparation with deeper research
- Develop more engaging illustrations
- Create age-appropriate teaching materials
- Generate thoughtful discussion questions

## Communications & Engagement

- Craft compelling content across all platforms
- Maintain consistent messaging
- Engage different generations effectively
- Build meaningful digital connections

## Worship Arts

- Design cohesive worship experiences
- Generate creative service elements
- Plan meaningful seasonal themes
- Support team collaboration

## Pastoral Care

- Create personalized care resources
- Develop support systems
- Generate follow-up frameworks
- Support counseling preparation

## Discipleship

- Design engaging small group materials
- Create growth pathways
- Develop leadership training
- Plan formation events

## Next Gen Ministry

- Generate youth and children's activities
- Create family ministry resources
- Design engaging events
- Support parent communication

## Outreach & Mission

- Plan community engagement
- Develop evangelism resources
- Create cultural connection points
- Support mission preparation

## Operations

- Streamline administrative tasks
- Create clear documentation
- Develop efficient systems
- Support team coordination

## How This Book Works

We've structured this resource to be immediately practical while building your long-term AI capabilities:

1. **Foundation First**: Chapter 1 provides essential AI concepts explained in ministry-relevant terms
2. **Role-Based Resources**: Each subsequent chapter focuses on a specific ministry area

3. **Ready-to-Use Prompts**: Every chapter includes customizable templates you can start using today
4. **Growth Path**: Advanced techniques help you expand your AI capabilities over time

Instead of getting lost in technical details, we focus on actionable prompts and real-world applications. Each chapter builds your confidence and competence in using AI tools while never losing sight of the ultimate goal: advancing God's kingdom and serving His people more effectively.

## Our Promise to You

This isn't about replacing human ministry with artificial intelligence. Instead, it's about empowering every ministry role with tools that multiply their impact. It's about freeing up more time for what matters most: personal connections, spiritual guidance, and kingdom building.

Whether you're leading a large congregation or serving a small community, this book will equip you to harness AI's potential in ways that enhance rather than diminish the personal nature of ministry.

## How to Use This Book

1. **Start with the Foundation**: Begin with Chapter 1 to build your AI understanding
2. **Focus on Your Role**: Jump to the chapters most relevant to your ministry area
3. **Begin Basic, Grow Advanced**: Start with simple prompts and gradually explore advanced techniques

4. **Practice and Refine**: Use the workshops to build your skills
5. **Reference as Needed**: Return to specific sections as new needs arise

Remember: Every prompt, technique, and strategy in this book is designed to serve one purpose—helping you share God's love more effectively in our rapidly changing world.

## The Journey Ahead

As we begin this journey together, hold onto this truth: AI is not replacing the heart of ministry. It's amplifying our ability to fulfill our calling. In the pages ahead, you'll discover practical ways to:

- Save time on routine tasks
- Enhance your creative processes
- Deepen your ministry preparation
- Strengthen your communication
- Multiply your impact

Most importantly, you'll learn how to keep Jesus at the center of everything—including how you use AI.

Let's begin this journey together, exploring how artificial intelligence can become a powerful tool in your ministry toolkit while maintaining the authentic, personal touch that makes ministry transformative.

The future of ministry is both human and AI-enhanced. Let's learn how to navigate it faithfully and effectively, always keeping our focus on what matters most—sharing God's love and building His kingdom.

# Chapter 1
## AI Essentials for Church Leaders

# Quick Overview

Think of AI as a helpful ministry assistant who has read every book ever written about church leadership and communications. This chapter will show you how to work with this assistant effectively. You'll learn how to give clear instructions (we call these "prompts") to get the help you need for your ministry tasks.

After reading this chapter, you'll be able to:

- Write clear prompts for common ministry tasks
- Get better results from AI tools
- Save time on routine communications
- Create more engaging content

# Core Concepts

### UNDERSTANDING AI AS YOUR MINISTRY ASSISTANT

AI is like having a knowledgeable volunteer who:

- Can help write newsletters, social posts, and emails
- Needs clear instructions to give you what you want
- Works best when you're specific about your church's context
- Should support, not replace, your ministry wisdom

## The Power of Good Prompts

A prompt is simply how you ask AI for help. The difference between a basic prompt and a great one is like the difference between asking someone to "help with the youth group" versus giving them a detailed ministry plan.

# Prompt Categories

## Ministry Communications Prompts

*Base Template for Church Content*

```
I am a [ROLE] at a [CHURCH SIZE/TYPE].

I need to create [CONTENT TYPE] for our
[EVENT/MINISTRY].

Our audience is [DESCRIBE AUDIENCE].


Please write content that:

1. Reflects our church's heart for [CORE
VALUE/MISSION]

2. Includes [SPECIFIC ELEMENTS]

3. Maintains a [TONE] tone

4. Is approximately [LENGTH]


Additional context:

- Key message: [MESSAGE]

- Important details: [DETAILS]

- Call to action: [WHAT YOU WANT PEOPLE TO DO]
```

*Quick Version*

    I am a [ROLE] at [CHURCH]. Write a [LENGTH]
    [CONTENT TYPE] about [TOPIC] for [AUDIENCE].
    Include [SPECIFIC NEEDS] and a clear next step.

## SERMON PREPARATION PROMPTS

*Base Template for Sermon Research*

    I am preparing a sermon on [PASSAGE] for our
    [CHURCH TYPE].

    Please help me with:

    1. Key themes and cross-references

    2. Modern application examples

    3. Potential illustrations

    4. Discussion questions


    Our congregation is primarily [DEMOGRAPHIC INFO].

    The main message I want to convey is [MESSAGE].

*Quick Version*

    Help me outline a sermon on [PASSAGE]. Focus on
    [THEME] and include 3 main points with
    applications.

## MINISTRY PLANNING PROMPTS

*Base Template for Event Planning*

```
I need to plan [EVENT TYPE] for our [MINISTRY].
Target audience: [WHO IT'S FOR]
Goals: [WHAT YOU WANT TO ACHIEVE]

Please provide:
1. Event outline
2. Promotion timeline
3. Volunteer needs
4. Budget considerations
5. Communication schedule
```

# Building Better Prompts

## ESSENTIAL COMPONENTS

1. Your Context
    - Church size and type
    - Ministry role
    - Target audience

2. Clear Expectations
    - Specific deliverables
    - Length requirements
    - Tone preferences
    - Key message

3. Ministry Purpose
    - Goals

- Values
- Desired outcomes

## Enhancement Tips

- Use chain of thought for complex decisions
- Add denominational context when relevant
- Specify your church's communication style
- Include any sensitive topics to avoid
- Mention specific ministry terminology you use

# Advanced Techniques

## Chain of Thought Prompting

Think of chain of thought prompting as walking with someone through a process step by step, just like you might disciple someone in their faith journey. Instead of asking AI to jump straight to the final answer, you guide it through the thinking process.

*Basic Template for Chain of Thought*

```
I am a [ROLE] at [CHURCH]. I need help with
[TASK].

Please think through this step by step:
1. First, consider [INITIAL CONSIDERATION]
2. Then, analyze [NEXT ELEMENT]
3. Next, evaluate [ADDITIONAL FACTOR]
4. Finally, create [FINAL OUTPUT]

For each step, share your thinking before moving
to the next step.
```

## Example: Sermon Series Planning

I am a teaching pastor at a suburban church of 500 people. I need to plan a 6-week sermon series on prayer.

Please think through this step by step:
1. First, consider our congregation's current understanding and practice of prayer
2. Then, analyze key biblical passages and themes about prayer
3. Next, evaluate how these themes connect to modern life challenges
4. Then, consider how to structure the series for spiritual growth
5. Finally, create a series outline with weekly topics

Share your thinking at each step before moving forward.

## Example: Ministry Decision

I am a youth pastor deciding whether to split our youth group by age. Walk through this decision with me.

Think through these steps:
1. First, list the key factors to consider (spiritual, social, practical)
2. Then, analyze the potential benefits of each approach
3. Next, evaluate possible challenges and solutions
4. Finally, recommend a path forward
Explain your reasoning at each step.

## Multi-Step Content Creation

    Step 1: "Create an outline for [CONTENT] that
    includes [ELEMENTS]"

    Step 2: "Using that outline, write a draft that
    emphasizes [KEY POINTS]"

    Step 3: "Review the draft and suggest improvements
    for [SPECIFIC ASPECTS]"

## Content Adaptation

    I need to adapt this [ORIGINAL CONTENT] for our
    [NEW PURPOSE].
    Original content: [PASTE CONTENT]
    New audience: [DESCRIBE AUDIENCE]
    New format: [SPECIFY FORMAT]
    Keep these key points: [LIST POINTS]

# Quick Start Prompts

## Newsletter Article

    I am the communications director at [CHURCH NAME],
    a [SIZE/TYPE] church.
    Write a newsletter article about our upcoming
    [EVENT].
    Length: 250 words
    Include: event details, why people should attend,
    how to register
    Tone: warm and inviting
    Target audience: church families with children

## Social Media Post

```
Create a Facebook post for our [MINISTRY EVENT].
Church context: [BRIEF DESCRIPTION]
Audience: [WHO NEEDS TO SEE THIS]
Include: key details, engaging hook, call to
action
Keep it: friendly, clear, and actionable
```

# Practice Workshop

## Exercise 1: Basic Prompt Writing

1. Take a current ministry need
2. Fill in the base template
3. Add your church's specific context
4. Test the prompt and refine

## Exercise 2: Content Adaptation

1. Choose a recent church announcement
2. Use the content adaptation prompt
3. Create versions for different platforms
4. Compare the results

# Next Steps

1. Start with the Quick Start prompts
2. Customize them for your church
3. Keep track of which prompts work best
4. Build your own prompt library

Remember: The best prompts are clear, specific, and grounded in your church's mission. Start simple and add detail as you get comfortable working with AI

# Chapter 2
## AI for Preaching and Teaching

## Quick Overview

AI tools like SermonSpark can transform your sermon preparation process, giving you more time to pray, reflect, and connect with your congregation. This chapter shows you how to use AI effectively while maintaining the spiritual integrity of your message.

You'll learn how to:

- Use AI to enhance (not replace) your sermon preparation
- Create powerful prompts for different sermon elements
- Save time on research and organization
- Develop more engaging illustrations and applications

## Core Concepts

### AI AS YOUR SERMON RESEARCH ASSISTANT

Think of AI as a research assistant who can:

- Find relevant verses and cross-references
- Generate sermon outline ideas
- Suggest illustrations and applications
- Help create supporting materials

But remember: AI supports your preparation; it doesn't replace prayer, personal study, or the Holy Spirit's guidance.

# Prompt Categories

## INITIAL RESEARCH PROMPTS

*Base Template for Passage Research*

```
I am preparing a sermon on [PASSAGE].
My congregation is [DESCRIBE CONGREGATION].
Key theme: [MAIN THEME]

Please help me understand:
1. Historical context
2. Key words and their meanings
3. Cross-references
4. Main theological themes

Format the response as a study outline.
```

*SermonSpark-Specific Tip*

Use SermonSpark's Research Tool to automatically gather cross-references and historical context. Then use this prompt to analyze and organize the findings.

## SERMON STRUCTURE PROMPTS

*Base Template for Sermon Outline*

```
Help me create a sermon outline for
[PASSAGE/TOPIC].
Sermon type: [EXPOSITORY/TOPICAL/NARRATIVE]
Time length: [MINUTES]
Main idea: [CENTRAL POINT]
```

```
Please provide:
1. Introduction approach
2. Main points (3-4)
3. Supporting scriptures
4. Potential transitions
5. Conclusion strategy
```

## Quick Outline Version

```
Create a [TIME]-minute sermon outline on
[PASSAGE].
Focus on [THEME].
Include 3 main points with supporting verses.
```

# ILLUSTRATION DEVELOPMENT

## Base Template for Illustrations

```
I need illustrations for a sermon on
[TOPIC/THEME].
My congregation includes [DEMOGRAPHICS].
Main point to illustrate: [POINT]

Please provide:
1. A modern-day parallel
2. A historical example
3. A familiar life situation
4. A possible object lesson

Each illustration should:
- Be relatable to [AUDIENCE]
- Connect clearly to [POINT]
- Take no more than 2 minutes to tell
```

## Application Generation

### Base Template for Applications

```
Help me develop applications for [SERMON POINT].
Congregation context: [DESCRIBE CONTEXT]
Main truth: [CORE TRUTH]

Create applications for:
1. Spiritual life
2. Family relationships
3. Work/School
4. Community impact

Each application should be:
- Specific and actionable
- Relevant to daily life
- Measurable in some way
```

# Advanced Techniques

## Chain of Thought for Sermon Development

```
I'm preparing a sermon on [PASSAGE]. Walk through
this process with me:

1. First, analyze the passage structure and
context
2. Then, identify the main theological themes
3. Next, consider our congregation's current needs
4. Then, develop potential applications
5. Finally, create an outline that connects text
to life

Explain your thinking at each step.
```

## SERIES PLANNING PROMPT

    I need to plan a [LENGTH] sermon series on
    [TOPIC/THEME].
    Congregation needs: [DESCRIBE NEEDS]
    Key objectives: [LIST OBJECTIVES]

    Please provide:
    1. Overall series arc
    2. Weekly themes
    3. Key passages
    4. Series graphics ideas
    5. Promotional concepts

# Time-Saving Strategies

## QUICK RESEARCH TEMPLATE

    I need quick insights on [PASSAGE] for [PURPOSE].
    Time available: [MINUTES]
    Focus areas:
    1. Main point
    2. Key cross-references
    3. One strong illustration
    4. Primary application

## SERMON SUPPORT MATERIALS

    Create supporting materials for my sermon on
    [TOPIC]:
    1. Small group questions
    2. Social media posts
    3. Bulletin summary
    4. Next steps card

```
Key message: [MESSAGE]
Target audience: [AUDIENCE]
```

# Practice Workshop

### Exercise 1: Research Prompt Development

1. Choose a passage
2. Write a research prompt
3. Analyze the results
4. Refine your prompt

### Exercise 2: Illustration Generation

1. Identify a key truth
2. Create an illustration prompt
3. Evaluate relevance
4. Adapt for your context

# Next Steps

- Start with the research prompts
- Build your outline library
- Create illustration templates
- Develop application frameworks

# Special SermonSpark Features

- Use the Title Generator for fresh perspectives
- Try the Outline Generator for quick structures
- Leverage the Verse Finder for connections
- Explore Social Media tools for sharing your message

Remember: AI tools enhance your preparation but don't replace the essential spiritual disciplines of prayer, study, and seeking the Holy Spirit's guidance.

# Chapter 3

## AI for Church Communications & Digital Engagement

# Quick Overview

Your church's message matters too much to get lost in the noise of modern communication. AI can help you share that message more effectively across every platform while maintaining authentic connections with your congregation.

You'll learn how to:

- Create consistent messages across multiple channels
- Save time on routine communications
- Engage different generations effectively
- Build meaningful connections through digital tools

# Core Concepts

### THE COMMUNICATIONS ECOSYSTEM

Think of your church's communication channels as different parts of one conversation:

- Sunday services build face-to-face connections
- Social media maintains daily engagement
- Email nurtures deeper relationships
- Website welcomes newcomers
- Print materials bridge digital divides

AI helps you maintain consistent messages across all these channels while speaking to each audience in their language.

## Prompt Categories

### MULTI-CHANNEL CONTENT CREATION

*Base Template for Content Adaptation*

```
I need to share [MESSAGE/ANNOUNCEMENT] across
multiple channels.
Church context: [DESCRIBE CHURCH]
Core message: [MAIN POINT]

Please create versions for:
1. Email newsletter (200-300 words)
2. Social media post (50 words)
3. Bulletin announcement (75 words)
4. Website update (150 words)
5. Digital display slide (25 words)

Each version should:
- Maintain our core message
- Adapt to the platform
- Include clear next steps
- Use appropriate tone
```

### SOCIAL MEDIA CONTENT

*Facebook Post Template*

```
Create a Facebook post for our [EVENT/MINISTRY].
Church type: [DESCRIBE CHURCH]
Target audience: [AUDIENCE]
Key message: [MESSAGE]
```

Include:
1. Attention-grabbing opening (max 15 words)
2. Event details (what, when, where)
3. Value proposition (why attend)
4. Call-to-action
5. Engaging question
6. Relevant hashtags (2-3)

Tone: Warm and inviting
Length: Short (100 words max)
```

## *Instagram Strategy Template*

```
Help me plan Instagram content for [EVENT/SERIES].
Church context: [CONTEXT]
Goal: [OBJECTIVE]

Create:
1. Main feed post
   - Caption (engaging, clear)
   - Hashtag suggestions
   - Call-to-action

2. Stories sequence (3-5 frames)
   - Key message points
   - Interactive elements
   - Swipe-up prompt

3. Engagement ideas
   - Poll questions
   - Discussion starters
   - Share prompts

# EMAIL COMMUNICATIONS

## Welcome Sequence Template

```
Design a 5-email welcome sequence for new
visitors.
Church details: [CHURCH INFO]
Target audience: [AUDIENCE]

For each email, provide:
1. Subject line (3 options)
2. Preview text
3. Main content (200 words)
4. Personal touch points
5. Clear next steps
6. Timing recommendation

Email themes:
1. Welcome and thank you
2. Our church story and values
3. Ways to get connected
4. Next steps in faith
5. Personal invitation
```

# CONTENT REPURPOSING

## Sermon to Social Template

```
Transform this sermon into social media content:
Sermon title: [TITLE]
Main points: [POINTS]
Scripture: [REFERENCES]
Target platforms: [PLATFORMS]

Create:
1. Main announcement post
2. 5 quote graphics with captions
```

```
3. 3 application points
4. 2 discussion questions
5. 1 behind-the-scenes insight
6. Weekly challenge post

Each piece should:
- Connect to the sermon
- Stand alone if needed
- Include relevant hashtags
- Drive engagement
```

## Advanced Techniques

### CHAIN OF THOUGHT FOR CAMPAIGN PLANNING

```
Help me plan a communication campaign for
[EVENT/INITIATIVE].
Walk through these steps:

1. First, analyze our audience segments and their
preferences
2. Then, identify key messages for each segment
3. Next, select appropriate channels for each
message
4. Then, develop content themes and hooks
5. Finally, create a content calendar

Explain your thinking at each step.
```

### PERSONALIZATION FRAMEWORK

```
Help me personalize this [CONTENT TYPE] for
different audiences:

Original message: [MESSAGE]
```

Audience segments:
1. Young families
2. Senior adults
3. Young professionals
4. Teens/students

For each segment, adapt:
- Language and tone
- Examples and references
- Call-to-action
- Platform choice

# Time-Saving Strategies

## Quick Response Templates

Create response templates for common situations:

1. First-time visitor follow-up
2. Prayer request acknowledgment
3. Ministry information request
4. Event registration confirmation
5. Volunteer interest response

Each template should:
- Be warm and personal
- Address specific needs
- Include next steps
- Maintain church voice

## Batch Content Creation

Generate a month of content for [MINISTRY]:

Theme: [MONTHLY THEME]

```
Key dates: [IMPORTANT DATES]
Platforms needed:
- Social media posts
- Email updates
- Bulletin announcements
- Website updates

For each piece:
- Align with theme
- Include key details
- Add engagement elements
- Maintain consistent voice
```

## Practice Workshop

### EXERCISE 1: PLATFORM ADAPTATION

1. Take one announcement
2. Create versions for each platform
3. Review for consistency
4. Test engagement elements

### EXERCISE 2: CAMPAIGN DEVELOPMENT

1. Choose an upcoming event
2. Plan multi-channel strategy
3. Create content templates
4. Set up measurement tools

## Next Steps

- Start with one platform
- Build your template library

- Test and refine your prompts
- Track engagement results

Remember: Technology serves your mission. Every post, email, or update should ultimately help people connect with God and your church community.

# Chapter 4

## AI for Worship Arts & Creative Planning

## Quick Overview

Creative planning for worship should flow from prayer and Spirit-led inspiration. AI can help streamline the technical aspects of creative planning, giving you more time to focus on seeking God's direction for your worship experiences.

You'll learn how to:

- Generate creative concepts that support your message
- Plan cohesive worship experiences
- Create visual elements that enhance worship
- Develop series themes that connect with your congregation

## Core Concepts

### AI as Your Creative Assistant

Think of AI as a creative brainstorming partner who can:

- Generate initial concepts to inspire your thinking
- Help organize creative elements
- Suggest visual directions
- Support technical planning

Remember: AI provides creative starting points; you provide the spiritual discernment and final creative direction.

# Prompt Categories

## SERMON SERIES CREATIVE DEVELOPMENT

*Base Template for Series Concept*

```
I need creative concepts for a sermon series on
[THEME/TOPIC].
Church context: [DESCRIBE CHURCH]
Series length: [NUMBER OF WEEKS]
Key message: [MAIN IDEA]

Please provide:
1. Series title options (5-7 ideas)
2. Visual theme concepts
   - Color palette suggestions
   - Imagery directions
   - Style approaches
3. Stage design elements
4. Graphics package needs
   - Social media
   - Environmental graphics
   - Print materials

The concepts should:
- Connect with [TARGET AUDIENCE]
- Support the biblical message
- Be feasible for our [RESOURCE LEVEL] resources
- Create a cohesive worship experience
```

## WORSHIP SERVICE PLANNING

*Service Flow Template*

```
Help me plan worship elements for [SERMON TOPIC].
Church style: [WORSHIP STYLE]
Service length: [TIME]
```

Theme: [THEME]

Create a service flow including:
1. Welcome/Opening elements
2. Worship set suggestions
   - Song progression
   - Scripture readings
   - Responsive elements
3. Transition moments
4. Creative elements
   - Video opportunities
   - Special moments
   - Interactive elements
5. Response time

Consider:
- Energy flow
- Thematic connection
- Congregational engagement
- Technical requirements

## STAGE DESIGN CONCEPTS

*Design Development Template*

Generate stage design concepts for [SERIES/SEASON].
Space details: [STAGE SPECIFICATIONS]
Budget level: [BUDGET RANGE]
Technical capabilities: [TECH SPECS]
Provide concepts that include:
1. Main design elements
2. Lighting suggestions
3. Digital elements
4. Material recommendations
5. Setup/transition plans

Each concept should:

- Support the message
- Be achievable with our resources
- Create meaningful atmosphere
- Allow for worship team spacing

# WORSHIP GRAPHICS PACKAGE

## Graphics Development Template

Create a graphics package plan for [SERIES/EVENT].
Style guide: [BRAND GUIDELINES]
Required elements:
1. Series graphics
2. Weekly titles
3. Worship backgrounds
4. Social media assets
5. Environmental graphics

For each element provide:
- Design direction
- Color schemes
- Typography suggestions
- Imagery concepts
- Production specifications

# Advanced Techniques

## CHAIN OF THOUGHT FOR CREATIVE PLANNING

```
Walk through the creative planning process for
[SERIES/EVENT]:

1. First, analyze the spiritual objectives
2. Then, explore creative directions that support
those goals
3. Next, consider practical implementation needs
4. Then, develop technical specifications
5. Finally, create production timeline

Explain the thinking at each step.
```

## MULTI-SENSORY EXPERIENCE DESIGN

```
Help me design a multi-sensory worship experience
for [THEME].
Service context: [SERVICE DETAILS]
Available elements:
- Visual capabilities
- Audio systems
- Environmental controls
- Physical space
- Interactive options

Design elements for:
1. Sight
2. Sound
3. Touch
4. Movement
5. Participation

Each element should:
```

- Enhance worship
- Support the message
- Create meaningful moments
- Be technically feasible

# Time-Saving Strategies

## Quick Creative Brief Template

```
Generate a creative brief for [PROJECT]:

1. Spiritual Objectives
   - Main message
   - Desired response
   - Biblical foundation

2. Creative Direction
   - Style approach
   - Key elements
   - Technical needs

3. Production Plan
   - Timeline
   - Resource needs
   - Team requirements
```

## Production Planning Template

```
Create a production plan for [EVENT/SERIES]:

Timeline:
- Planning milestones
- Design deadlines
- Production schedule
- Setup requirements
```

```
- Rehearsal needs

Team needs:
- Creative roles
- Technical positions
- Volunteer support
- Schedule coordination
```

## Practice Workshop

### EXERCISE 1: SERIES DEVELOPMENT

1. Choose a sermon series
2. Generate creative concepts
3. Develop visual direction
4. Plan implementation

### EXERCISE 2: SERVICE FLOW

1. Select a worship theme
2. Create service elements
3. Plan transitions
4. Design technical cues

## Next Steps

- Start with series planning
- Build your creative library
- Develop production templates
- Create team workflows

Remember: Technology and creativity serve worship; they don't define it. Every creative element should point people to Jesus and create space for genuine worship experiences.

# Chapter 5

## AI for Congregational Care & Counseling

## Quick Overview

In ministry, nothing replaces the power of personal presence and pastoral care. While AI can't replicate these sacred connections, it can help you create thoughtful resources and systems that support your caring ministry, giving you more time for those vital personal interactions that truly matter.

You'll learn how to:

- Create personalized care resources that speak to specific needs
- Develop consistent follow-up systems that ensure no one falls through the cracks
- Build comprehensive care guides for your ministry team
- Generate supportive content for life's challenging moments

## Core Concepts

### AI AS YOUR PASTORAL CARE ASSISTANT

Think of AI as a behind-the-scenes ministry partner who can:

- Help draft initial care messages
- Generate prayer and devotional content
- Create resource libraries
- Support administrative tasks

Remember: AI provides resources and frameworks; you provide the personal touch and pastoral wisdom that make care meaningful.

# Prompt Categories

## Personalized Care Communication

*Base Template for Care Messages*

```
Help me craft a pastoral care message for
[SITUATION].
Church context: [CHURCH INFO]
Recipient context: [SITUATION DETAILS]
Relationship: [CONNECTION LEVEL]

Create a message that:
1. Expresses genuine care
2. Offers specific support
3. Includes relevant scripture
4. Provides clear next steps
5. Opens door for conversation

Tone: Warm, pastoral, authentic
Length: [SPECIFY LENGTH]
Include: Prayer or blessing
```

## Prayer and Devotional Content

*Custom Devotional Template*

```
Create a personalized devotional for someone
facing [SITUATION].
Length: 5 days
Focus: [SPIRITUAL THEME]
Current need: [SPECIFIC NEED]
```

For each day provide:
1. Scripture passage
2. Brief reflection (150 words)
3. Personal application
4. Prayer prompt
5. Encouraging thought

Style:
- Compassionate tone
- Relatable examples
- Hope-filled perspective
- Practical applications

## CARE RESOURCE DEVELOPMENT

### Support Guide Template

```
Develop a care resource for [LIFE SITUATION].
Purpose: [INTENDED USE]
Audience: [WHO IT'S FOR]

Include:
1. Understanding the Situation
    - Common experiences
    - Normal reactions
    - Warning signs

2. Spiritual Support
    - Relevant scriptures
    - Prayer guidance
    - Faith perspectives

3. Practical Help
    - Action steps
    - Support resources
    - Professional referrals

4. Care Team Guidelines
```

- How to help
- What to say/not say
- When to escalate

# CRISIS RESPONSE FRAMEWORK

## *Crisis Communication Template*

```
Help me create a crisis response framework for
[SITUATION TYPE].
Church size: [CONGREGATION SIZE]
Resources available: [SUPPORT SYSTEMS]

Develop:
1. Initial Response
    - First 24 hours
    - Communication plan
    - Support mobilization

2. Ongoing Care
    - Follow-up schedule
    - Resource deployment
    - Care team roles

3. Long-term Support
    - Transition plans
    - Community resources
    - Healing pathways

Include templates for:
- Staff notifications
- Congregation updates
- Family communication
- Prayer requests
```

# Advanced Techniques

## CHAIN OF THOUGHT FOR CARE PLANNING

```
Walk through care planning for [SITUATION]:

1. First, assess immediate needs and support
systems
2. Then, identify spiritual care opportunities
3. Next, develop practical support strategies
4. Then, create communication touchpoints
5. Finally, establish long-term care plans

Explain the pastoral approach at each step.
```

## CUSTOMIZED CARE PATHWAYS

```
Design a care pathway for [LIFE SITUATION]:

Journey stages:
1. Initial Contact
    - First response
    - Resource sharing
    - Next steps

2. Active Support
    - Regular check-ins
    - Group connections
    - Resource access

3. Ongoing Care
    - Follow-up schedule
    - Growth opportunities
    - Community integration

For each stage, include:
```

```
- Communication templates
- Resource recommendations
- Ministry connections
- Progress indicators
```

## Next Steps

- Start with simple response templates
- Build your resource library gradually
- Develop care pathways as needed
- Create team training materials

Remember: Technology supports ministry; it doesn't replace it. Every message, resource, or guide should ultimately help people experience God's love through personal pastoral care.

# Chapter 6

## AI for Discipleship & Small Group Ministry

## Quick Overview

Discipleship is about walking alongside people in their spiritual journey. While AI can't replace the relational heart of discipleship, it can help you create more intentional pathways and resources that support deeper spiritual growth in your community.

You'll learn how to:

- Design engaging small group materials
- Create personalized growth pathways
- Develop leadership training resources
- Plan meaningful spiritual formation events

## Core Concepts

### AI AS YOUR DISCIPLESHIP ASSISTANT

Think of AI as a ministry partner who can:

- Help structure spiritual growth content
- Generate discussion questions that spark meaningful conversation

- Create customized growth plans
- Support leadership development

Remember: AI provides frameworks and content starting points; authentic discipleship happens through Spirit-led relationships and community.

# Prompt Categories

## SMALL GROUP RESOURCE DEVELOPMENT

*Discussion Guide Template*

```
Create a small group guide for [PASSAGE/TOPIC].
Group type: [GROUP DESCRIPTION]
Meeting length: [TIME]
Spiritual maturity: [LEVEL]

Include:
1. Ice Breaker (5-10 minutes)
   - Connection to theme
   - Easy participation
   - Group building

2. Scripture Exploration (20-30 minutes)
   - Key passages
   - Context insights
   - Discussion questions
   - Application points

3. Life Application (15-20 minutes)
   - Personal reflection
   - Group discussion
   - Action steps
   - Prayer focus
```

4. Leader Notes
   - Preparation tips
   - Discussion guidance
   - Potential challenges
   - Follow-up suggestions

# PERSONALIZED GROWTH PATHWAYS

## *Spiritual Growth Plan Template*

```
Design a growth pathway for [PERSON
TYPE/SITUATION].
Current stage: [SPIRITUAL MATURITY]
Areas for growth: [KEY AREAS]
Available resources: [CHURCH PROGRAMS]

Create a 3-month plan including:
1. Weekly Focus Areas
    - Scripture reading
    - Prayer practices
    - Study resources
    - Community engagement

2. Growth Markers
    - Knowledge goals
    - Practice objectives
    - Community involvement
    - Service opportunities

3. Support Elements
    - Accountability suggestions
    - Resource recommendations
    - Connection points
    - Challenge activities
```

## LEADERSHIP DEVELOPMENT

*Leader Training Module Template*

```
Develop a training module for [LEADERSHIP ROLE].
Ministry context: [MINISTRY AREA]
Experience level: [LEADER LEVEL]
Time frame: [TRAINING DURATION]

Create content for:
1. Core Competencies
    - Biblical foundations
    - Leadership principles
    - Practical skills
    - Ministry specifics

2. Training Elements
    - Teaching content
    - Discussion questions
    - Role-play scenarios
    - Assessment tools

3. Growth Exercises
    - Reflection activities
    - Practice opportunities
    - Feedback loops
    - Mentoring guides
```

## RETREAT AND EVENT PLANNING

*Event Design Template*

```
Help me plan a [EVENT TYPE] for [TARGET GROUP].
Theme: [MAIN FOCUS]
Duration: [TIME FRAME]
Location type: [VENUE]
```

```
Develop:
1. Program Flow
   - Session themes
   - Activity sequence
   - Discussion formats
   - Spiritual elements

2. Activity Options
   - Group exercises
   - Individual reflection
   - Creative elements
   - Community building

3. Resource Needs
   - Materials list
   - Space requirements
   - Leader preparation
   - Participant guides
```

# Advanced Techniques

## CHAIN OF THOUGHT FOR DISCIPLESHIP PLANNING

```
Walk through discipleship planning for
[GROUP/INDIVIDUAL]:

1. First, assess current spiritual maturity and
needs
2. Then, identify key growth areas and goals
3. Next, develop specific learning objectives
4. Then, create engagement strategies
5. Finally, establish progress markers

Explain your discipleship approach at each step.
```

## Multi-Generation Ministry Design

```
Create a ministry strategy that engages multiple
generations:

Target groups:
1. Gen Z (teens/young adults)
2. Millennials
3. Gen X
4. Boomers
5. Silent Generation

For each group, develop:
- Learning approaches
- Connection points
- Growth activities
- Leadership opportunities
- Service engagement

Consider:
- Communication preferences
- Learning styles
- Life stage needs
- Technology comfort
- Ministry interests
```

# Time-Saving Tools

## Quick Discussion Starter Template

```
Generate discussion starters for [TOPIC/PASSAGE]:

1. Opening Questions
   - Ice breaker
   - Connection point
   - Personal reflection
```

2. Deep Dive Questions
   - Biblical exploration
   - Life application
   - Group interaction

3. Action Questions
   - Next steps
   - Accountability
   - Prayer focus

## LEADERSHIP RESOURCE LIBRARY

Create a resource collection for [MINISTRY AREA]:

Include:
1. Quick Reference Guides
   - Key principles
   - Best practices
   - Common challenges

2. Training Materials
   - Core competencies
   - Skill development
   - Growth pathways

3. Ministry Tools
   - Planning templates
   - Assessment resources
   - Follow-up guides

# Next Steps

- Start with basic discussion guides
- Build your resource library
- Develop leadership pathways
- Create growth frameworks

Remember: Technology serves discipleship; it doesn't drive it. Every resource, plan, or guide should ultimately help people grow closer to Jesus through authentic community and personal transformation.

# Chapter 7

## AI for Next Gen Ministry: Youth & Children

## Quick Overview

Ministry to young people is all about authentic connection and engaging presentation. While AI can't replace your heart for the next generation, it can help you create dynamic, age-appropriate resources that speak their language and capture their imagination.

You'll learn how to:

- Design engaging lessons that connect with different age groups
- Create resources that bridge church and home
- Plan dynamic events that draw young people closer to Jesus
- Develop materials that make faith come alive

## Core Concepts

### AI as Your Next Gen Ministry Assistant

Think of AI as a creative ministry partner who can:

- Generate fresh activity ideas
- Create age-appropriate content

- Support parent communication
- Help plan engaging events

Remember: AI provides creative starting points; you provide the relational connection and spiritual mentoring that transforms young lives.

# Prompt Categories

## YOUTH LESSON DEVELOPMENT

*Youth Bible Study Template*

```
Create a youth lesson for [PASSAGE/TOPIC].
Age group: [AGE RANGE]
Time frame: [DURATION]
Ministry setting: [CONTEXT]

Include:
1. Hook/Opening (10 minutes)
   - Attention grabber
   - Topic connection
   - Group interaction

2. Book/Bible Exploration (20 minutes)
   - Key scripture insights
   - Modern applications
   - Discussion questions
   - Media tie-ins

3. Look/Application (15 minutes)
   - Real-life scenarios
   - Group activities
   - Personal challenges
   - Social media connections
```

4. Took/Response (10 minutes)
      - Creative response
      - Action steps
      - Prayer focus
      - Take-home challenge

Additional elements:
- Parent connection point
- Social media prompts
- Group text ideas
- Follow-up suggestions

# CHILDREN'S MINISTRY RESOURCES

## Kid's Lesson Template

Design a children's lesson for [TOPIC].
Age level: [AGE GROUP]
Time: [DURATION]
Theme: [MAIN POINT]

Create:
1. Welcome Activity (5-10 minutes)
   - Energy level: [HIGH/MEDIUM/LOW]
   - Supply needs
   - Setup instructions
   - Connection to lesson

2. Bible Story Presentation (10-15 minutes)
   - Story breakdown
   - Interactive elements
   - Visual aids
   - Memory verse

3. Learning Activities (20 minutes)
   - Craft project
   - Game ideas
   - Object lesson

- Small group options

4. Family Connection
    - Take-home sheet
    - Parent prompts
    - Weekly challenge
    - Family discussion starters

# FAMILY MINISTRY RESOURCES

## *Family Devotional Template*

```
Create a family devotional series on [THEME].
Target age range: [AGES]
Format: [DAILY/WEEKLY]
Length: [DURATION]

Develop:
1. Daily/Weekly Structure
    - Bible reading
    - Discussion starters
    - Activity options
    - Prayer focus

2. Parent Guides
    - Age adaptations
    - Conversation tips
    - Teachable moments
    - Further resources

3. Creative Elements
    - Family challenges
    - Service projects
    - Memory activities
    - Media connections

Make it:
- Easy to implement
```

- Flexible for different schedules
- Engaging for all ages
- Social media friendly

## EVENT PLANNING

### Youth Event Template

```
Help me plan a [EVENT TYPE] for [AGE GROUP].
Theme: [FOCUS]
Duration: [TIME]
Location: [VENUE TYPE]

Design:
1. Event Flow
    - Schedule outline
    - Activity rotation
    - Energy management
    - Space utilization

2. Program Elements
    - Welcome/intro
    - Main activities
    - Small groups
    - Worship elements
    - Teaching time
    - Response moments

3. Engagement Strategy
    - Social media plan
    - Photo opportunities
    - Group interaction
    - Follow-up ideas

4. Promotion Plan
    - Announcement timeline
    - Graphics needs
```

```
- Social strategy
- Parent communication
```

# Advanced Techniques

## CHAIN OF THOUGHT FOR AGE-APPROPRIATE TEACHING

```
Help me adapt this message for different age
groups:

Original concept: [TEACHING POINT]

Walk through adaptation for:
1. Preschool (3-5)
   - Key phrase
   - Simple activity
   - Visual help

2. Elementary (6-11)
   - Main idea
   - Interactive elements
   - Take-home point

3. Middle School (12-14)
   - Core truth
   - Discussion approach
   - Life application

4. High School (15-18)
   - Deep dive
   - Cultural connection
   - Personal challenge

Explain your thinking for each adaptation.
```

## MULTI-GENERATION EVENT DESIGN

```
Plan a family ministry event that engages all
ages:

Event focus: [THEME/PURPOSE]
Expected attendance: [NUMBER]
Space available: [VENUE DETAILS]

Create activities for:
1. Preschool Zone
     - Active games
     - Craft station
     - Story corner

2. Elementary Area
     - Team challenges
     - Discovery stations
     - Creative space

3. Teen Space
     - Hangout area
     - Discussion pods
     - Service projects

4. Family Together Time
     - Group activities
     - Worship moments
     - Shared experiences

Include:
- Cross-age interactions
- Parent engagement
- Photo opportunities
- Take-home elements
```

## Next Steps

- Start with basic lesson templates
- Build your activity library
- Develop parent resources
- Create event frameworks

Remember: Technology supports ministry; it doesn't drive it. Every resource, event, or activity should ultimately help young people and families experience Jesus in relevant, transformative ways.

# Chapter 8
## AI for Outreach & Missions Strategies

## Quick Overview

Effective outreach starts with understanding your community and sharing God's love in relevant ways. While AI can't replace authentic relationships in missions and evangelism, it can help you develop strategic approaches that connect with people where they are.

You'll learn how to:

- Design impactful community outreach initiatives
- Create culturally sensitive mission resources
- Develop strategic partnership opportunities
- Plan meaningful evangelistic engagement

## Core Concepts

### AI AS YOUR OUTREACH STRATEGIST

Think of AI as a research and planning partner who can:

- Help identify community needs
- Generate creative outreach ideas
- Support cultural understanding
- Assist with strategic planning

Remember: AI provides insights and frameworks; authentic connection and Spirit-led evangelism drive real transformation.

# Prompt Categories

## COMMUNITY OUTREACH PLANNING

*Event Strategy Template*

```
Help me design an outreach event for [COMMUNITY
TYPE].
Church context: [CHURCH INFO]
Target audience: [DEMOGRAPHIC]
Available resources: [RESOURCES]

Develop a plan including:
1. Event Concept
   - Theme/focus
   - Unique value proposition
   - Community benefit
   - Connection points

2. Implementation Strategy
   - Timeline
   - Resource needs
   - Volunteer roles
   - Partner opportunities

3. Communication Plan
   - Marketing channels
   - Key messages
   - Community outreach
   - Follow-up strategy

4. Impact Measurement
   - Success metrics
   - Follow-up process
   - Long-term connection
   - Growth opportunities
```

# EVANGELISM RESOURCE DEVELOPMENT

## *Conversation Guide Template*

```
Create evangelism resources for
[CONTEXT/AUDIENCE].
Cultural background: [CULTURE INFO]
Common questions: [LIST QUESTIONS]
Ministry setting: [SETTING]

Include:
1. Conversation Starters
   - Natural opening points
   - Cultural connections
   - Relevant topics
   - Bridge-building questions

2. Faith Story Framework
   - Personal testimony tips
   - Scripture integration
   - Cultural sensitivity
   - Response guidance

3. Follow-up Resources
   - Next step options
   - Study materials
   - Community connections
   - Growth pathways
```

# COMMUNITY RESEARCH

## *Needs Assessment Template*

```
Help me research community needs in
[AREA/DEMOGRAPHIC].
Focus areas:
1. Demographics
```

2. Social needs
3. Economic factors
4. Cultural context

Analyze:
1. Current Landscape
    - Population data
    - Social indicators
    - Economic trends
    - Cultural factors

2. Ministry Opportunities
    - Service gaps
    - Partnership potential
    - Resource alignment
    - Impact areas

3. Action Strategy
    - Priority needs
    - Church resources
    - Implementation steps
    - Success metrics

# Mission Trip Planning

## *Cross-Cultural Guide Template*

```
Develop a mission trip guide for
[LOCATION/CULTURE].
Trip duration: [LENGTH]
Team size: [NUMBER]
Ministry focus: [PURPOSE]

Create:
1. Cultural Preparation
    - Cultural overview
    - Language basics
    - Customs/traditions
    - Do's and don'ts

2. Ministry Training
    - Context understanding
    - Service approaches
    - Team dynamics
    - Spiritual preparation

3. Practical Resources
    - Daily schedules
    - Team devotionals
    - Communication tips
    - Safety guidelines

4. Follow-up Framework
    - Debrief guides
    - Story sharing
    - Partnership maintenance
    - Long-term impact
```

# Advanced Techniques

## CHAIN OF THOUGHT FOR COMMUNITY ENGAGEMENT

```
Walk through community engagement strategy for
[INITIATIVE]:

1. First, analyze community context and needs
2. Then, identify connection points and
opportunities
3. Next, develop engagement approaches
4. Then, create implementation plan
5. Finally, establish impact measurement

Explain your strategic thinking at each step.
```

## MULTI-CULTURAL MINISTRY DESIGN

```
Design a cross-cultural ministry strategy:

Target cultures:
1. [CULTURE 1]
2. [CULTURE 2]
3. [CULTURE 3]

For each culture, develop:
1. Connection Strategy
    - Cultural bridges
    - Natural gatherings
    - Common interests
    - Service opportunities

2. Communication Plan
    - Language considerations
    - Cultural values
    - Message framing
```

```
    - Media choices

3. Ministry Approach
    - Relationship building
    - Service projects
    - Spiritual conversations
    - Growth pathways
```

## Next Steps

- Start with community research
- Build your outreach library
- Develop partnership strategies
- Create cultural guides

Remember: Technology supports outreach; relationships drive transformation. Every strategy, event, or resource should ultimately help people experience God's love through authentic community connection.

# Chapter 9

## AI for Church Operations & Administration

## Quick Overview

Effective church administration creates the foundation for thriving ministry. While AI can't replace the human touch in church operations, it can help you create efficient systems that free your team to focus on what matters most - serving people and advancing your church's mission.

You'll learn how to:

- Create clear, actionable administrative documents
- Develop people-focused processes and procedures
- Design efficient operational workflows
- Build meaningful connection pathways

## Core Concepts

### AI AS YOUR ADMINISTRATIVE PARTNER

Think of AI as an operations assistant who can:

- Draft clear documentation
- Structure efficient processes
- Support visitor connections
- Enhance team communication

Remember: AI provides administrative frameworks; your church's heart and mission guide how you implement them.

# Prompt Categories

## MEETING MANAGEMENT

*Meeting Documentation Template*

```
Help me create documents for [MEETING TYPE].
Church context: [CHURCH INFO]
Participants: [ATTENDEE ROLES]
Meeting purpose: [OBJECTIVE]

Generate:
1. Agenda Template
    - Opening elements
    - Key discussion points
    - Decision items
    - Next steps
    - Prayer focus

2. Minutes Framework
    - Attendance tracking
    - Discussion highlights
    - Action items
    - Follow-up assignments
    - Resource needs

3. Follow-up Template
    - Decision summary
    - Task assignments
    - Timeline tracking
    - Resource allocation
    - Prayer requests
```

# ROLE DEVELOPMENT

## *Ministry Position Template*

```
Create a comprehensive description for [ROLE].
Ministry area: [DEPARTMENT]
Type: [STAFF/VOLUNTEER]
Time commitment: [HOURS]

Include:
1. Role Overview
    - Purpose statement
    - Ministry impact
    - Key responsibilities
    - Success measures

2. Requirements
    - Spiritual qualities
    - Skills needed
    - Time expectations
    - Training provided

3. Growth Path
    - Onboarding process
    - Development opportunities
    - Mentoring connections
    - Leadership pathway

4. Support Framework
    - Resources provided
    - Team connection
    - Accountability structure
    - Recognition plan
```

# Policy and Procedure Development

## Church Policy Template

```
Develop a policy for [AREA/TOPIC].
Church size: [CONGREGATION SIZE]
Ministry context: [CONTEXT]
Key stakeholders: [ROLES]

Create:
1. Policy Framework
    - Purpose statement
    - Biblical foundation
    - Scope and application
    - Key definitions

2. Procedure Details
    - Step-by-step process
    - Role responsibilities
    - Decision points
    - Exception handling

3. Implementation Guide
    - Training needs
    - Communication plan
    - Timeline
    - Success metrics

Make it:
- Clear and actionable
- Ministry-minded
- People-focused
- Legally sound
```

# VISITOR CONNECTION SYSTEM

## *Welcome Process Template*

```
Design a visitor follow-up system for our church.
Church size: [SIZE]
Current process: [CURRENT APPROACH]
Available resources: [RESOURCES]

Develop:
1. Initial Welcome
    - First contact timing
    - Communication channels
    - Welcome resources
    - Next step options

2. Connection Pathway
    - Follow-up sequence
    - Ministry introductions
    - Community opportunities
    - Growth options

3. Integration Steps
    - Membership path
    - Ministry involvement
    - Small group connection
    - Serving opportunities

4. Measurement Tools
    - Tracking systems
    - Success indicators
    - Follow-up points
    - Feedback loops
```

# Advanced Techniques

## CHAIN OF THOUGHT FOR PROCESS DEVELOPMENT

```
Walk through process development for [MINISTRY
AREA]:

1. First, identify current pain points and needs
2. Then, map ideal workflow and outcomes
3. Next, develop specific process steps
4. Then, create support documentation
5. Finally, establish training and implementation

Explain your operational thinking at each step.
```

## MULTI-DEPARTMENT INTEGRATION

```
Design a cross-ministry workflow for [PROCESS]:

Departments involved:
1. [DEPARTMENT 1]
2. [DEPARTMENT 2]
3. [DEPARTMENT 3]

For each department:
1. Role Definition
    - Responsibilities
    - Decision authority
    - Resource needs
    - Communication paths

2. Process Integration
    - Workflow touchpoints
    - Handoff procedures
    - Quality checks
    - Timeline markers
```

3. Success Measures
   - Key metrics
   - Review points
   - Feedback loops
   - Improvement process

## Next Steps

- Start with core documentation
- Build your process library
- Develop role guides
- Create connection systems

Remember: Technology supports ministry operations; people drive ministry impact. Every system, process, or document should ultimately help your church serve people more effectively and advance your mission with excellence.

# Chapter 10

## Bringing It All Together - Your Church's AI Journey

Throughout this book, we've explored the transformative potential of AI across every aspect of ministry. From crafting compelling sermons to nurturing your congregation, from reaching new people to streamlining operations, we've seen how AI can enhance your church's ability to share God's love and build meaningful connections.

But now comes perhaps the most challenging part of the journey: turning all these possibilities into reality in your unique church context.

## The Integration Challenge

Picture your church's current technology landscape. Maybe you have some staff members already experimenting with AI tools, while others remain hesitant. Perhaps you're seeing redundant subscriptions across departments, or wondering how to create policies that balance innovation with wisdom. You might even be concerned about the time and resources required to implement all these new possibilities effectively.

These are the exact challenges we see churches facing every day. The path to effective AI integration involves far more than just choosing the right tools – it requires orchestrating a transformation that touches every area of ministry.

## Understanding Where You Are

Before you can chart a course forward, you need a clear picture of your starting point. This means taking a deep dive into your current technology ecosystem: What tools are already in use? How are they being used? Where are the gaps and opportunities? More importantly, how does your team feel about these technologies?

Maria, a communications director at a mid-sized church, recently shared her experience: "I knew we needed to embrace AI, but when I started documenting our current tech stack, I discovered we had three different AI writing tools, two image generators, and various other subscriptions – all being used in isolation. Just getting a handle on what we had was overwhelming."

## The Implementation Mountain

Once you understand your current landscape, the real work begins. You're looking at developing comprehensive implementation plans, creating new policies, designing training programs, and managing change across your entire organization. Each step requires careful consideration:

Do you have the right people in place to champion this transformation? How will you train staff and volunteers effectively? What about security and ethical considerations? How do you ensure AI enhances rather than replaces the human touch in ministry?

Think of it like renovating your church building while services are still happening – it requires careful planning, clear communication, and a lot of patience.

## The Reality Check

Let's be honest: implementing AI effectively in your church requires hundreds of hours of assessment and planning. You're looking at extensive documentation and policy creation, continuous training and support, ongoing maintenance and updates, regular evaluation and adjustment, and constant communication and coordination.

For most churches, this level of investment simply isn't feasible alongside the daily demands of ministry. Your time and energy are better spent focusing on what matters most – ministering to your community and sharing God's love.

## A Better Way Forward

This is exactly why we created the AI LaunchPoint Consultation. We've taken everything we've learned about effective AI integration in churches and created a streamlined process that helps you implement these tools without the overwhelming complexity.

Think of it as having an experienced guide for your AI journey – someone who knows the terrain, understands the challenges, and can help you navigate the path efficiently.

Here's how it works:

Instead of spending months trying to figure everything out on your own, our team of church technology experts will:

- Assess where your staff currently are with AI
- Identify and eliminate redundant tools
- Create or update your AI policies
- Develop a clear action plan

- Provide initial training
- Guide you through implementation

All of this happens through a proven process that takes weeks instead of months.

# Your Next Step

As we conclude this book, you have two paths before you. You can begin the complex journey of AI integration on your own, investing significant time and resources in figuring everything out from scratch. Or you can partner with our team at AI for Churches, leveraging our experience and proven process to implement these tools efficiently and effectively.

Your mission is too important to let technology challenges slow you down. Visit AI-for-Churches.com today to schedule a free 30-minute discovery call. Let's talk about how we can help you harness the power of AI to enhance your ministry while staying focused on what matters most – sharing God's love with your community.

Remember, technology isn't the end goal – it's a tool to help you fulfill your mission more effectively. Whether you choose to partner with us or move forward on your own, stay focused on using these powerful new tools to build genuine connections and transform lives through the power of the gospel.

# Appendix

## Recommended AI Resources for Church Leaders

The journey of integrating AI into your ministry doesn't end with this book – it's just beginning. We've curated this collection of resources to help you continue growing, learning, and connecting with others who share your vision for innovative ministry.

## Essential AI Tools for Ministry

### CONTENT CREATION AND MINISTRY SUPPORT

- **SermonSpark** (sermonspark.ai) Our purpose-built tool for sermon preparation and ministry content creation, designed by church leaders for church leaders.
- **ChatGPT** (chat.openai.com) Perfect for general content creation and administrative tasks, with both free and premium options.
- **Claude** (anthropic.com) Excellent for deeper research and theological discussions, with strong analytical capabilities.

### VISUAL MINISTRY TOOLS

- **Adobe Firefly** Create ministry-appropriate images with ethical AI generation.
- **Canva with AI Features** Design church graphics with integrated AI assistance.

## Ministry Operations

- **Notion AI** Streamline church documentation and team collaboration.
- **Otter.ai** Transform sermons and meetings into searchable text.

# Must-Read Books

**AI and the Church: A Clear Guide for the Curious and Courageous** by Jason Moore

This groundbreaking guide tackles the critical questions churches face about AI implementation. Moore provides both practical insights and theological wisdom, helping leaders see AI not as a threat but as a powerful tool for ministry. The book covers everything from basic concepts to cutting-edge applications, always keeping the church's mission at the center.

**The Church and AI: Seven Guidelines for Ministry on the Digital Frontiers** by David Betts

Betts offers seven essential guidelines for ministry in the age of AI, addressing crucial questions about leadership, pastoral care, and church-wide implementation. This thoughtful exploration helps churches move from reactive to proactive in their AI approach, providing clear pathways for faithful innovation.

# Join the Community

## AI for Churches Facebook Group

Step into a vibrant community of ministry innovators at facebook.com/groups/aiforchurches. Here you'll find:

- Daily discussions about AI in ministry
- Real-world implementation stories
- Quick answers to your questions
- Connections with forward-thinking church leaders

## Monthly Cohorts

Join a community of learners in our interactive monthly cohorts, where you'll:

- Master practical AI skills alongside other church leaders
- Get hands-on experience with key tools
- Build relationships with innovative ministry peers
- Develop your church's AI strategy
- Access exclusive resources and support

# Stay Connected

## Digital Resources

- **AI for Churches Blog** Fresh insights and implementation tips at ai-for-churches.com/blog

# Ongoing Support

## AI for Churches Resource Center

Access tools for your journey at https://ai-for-churches.com:

- Implementation guides
- Policy templates
- Training materials
- Best practice documents
- Case studies

## Getting Help

We're here to support your AI ministry journey:

1. **Join the Community** Connect with peers in our Facebook group
2. **Learn Together** Grow through our monthly cohorts
3. **Access Resources** Explore our online resource library
4. **Get Personal Guidance** Consider our AI LaunchPoint consultation

# Looking Forward

The landscape of AI and ministry will continue evolving, but our mission remains constant: helping churches leverage technology to share God's love more effectively. Stay connected with the AI for Churches community to keep learning and growing together.

Visit https://ai-for-churches.com to:

- Join our Facebook community
- Enroll in upcoming cohorts

- Access our resource library
- Schedule a consultation

Remember, technology is simply a tool to enhance, not replace, the vital personal connections that drive ministry impact. Together, we can harness these new capabilities while staying focused on what matters most – sharing the timeless message of Jesus in relevant, transformative ways.

# About the Authors

### THE HEART BEHIND THIS BOOK

Before we introduce ourselves, we want to share why we wrote this book. In our years of working with churches, we've witnessed both the excitement and uncertainty that AI brings to ministry. We've seen the transformative potential of these tools, but also understand the very real concerns church leaders face when considering their implementation.

This book emerged from countless conversations with pastors and ministry leaders who were asking the same questions: How can we use AI effectively while staying true to our mission? How do we navigate the ethical implications? How do we implement these tools in ways that enhance rather than replace genuine ministry connections?

Our goal wasn't just to write another technology book – we wanted to create a practical guide that would help church leaders confidently step into the future of ministry while keeping their focus firmly on what matters most: sharing God's love and building authentic community

# Meet Your Guides

## Katie Allred, MA

Katie is more than just a marketing strategist and communications expert – she's a passionate advocate for helping churches share their message effectively in our digital age. With deep expertise in content strategy, website development, and emerging technologies, Katie has dedicated her career to empowering ministry leaders to create meaningful connections through strategic communication.

Known for her ability to make complex concepts accessible, Katie brings a unique blend of technical knowledge and practical ministry understanding to her work. Her workshops and consulting sessions have helped countless church leaders embrace new technologies while staying true to their mission.

Katie's philosophy is simple: technology should serve ministry, not complicate it. This belief drives her approach to helping churches leverage AI and other digital tools in ways that enhance their ability to reach people with the gospel.

## David Thorne, Ed.D.

As the leader of the AI for Churches, David brings a rare combination of pastoral heart and technological insight to the conversation about AI in ministry. With a doctorate in Leadership Studies and masters degrees in management and leadership, counseling, and practical theology, he understands both the technical and spiritual dimensions of implementing AI in church contexts.

David's passion for helping pastors optimize their sermon writing process while maintaining authenticity comes from his own experience as a pastor and family man.

He deeply understands the challenges church leaders face in our rapidly changing world and is committed to helping them navigate these changes without losing sight of their calling.

His focus on ethical AI implementation ensures that churches can embrace these powerful tools while maintaining the integrity of their ministry.

# The AI for Churches Community

This book is just the beginning of your journey. We invite you to join the vibrant community of ministry leaders who are learning, growing, and innovating together:

- **Connect with Us**: Join our Facebook group at facebook.com/groups/aiforchurches
- **Learn Together**: Participate in our monthly cohorts
- **Get Resources**: Access implementation guides at ai-for-churches.com
- **Stay Updated**: Follow our blog and YouTube channel for the latest insights

# Our Invitation to You

We believe that the future of ministry holds incredible opportunities for churches that thoughtfully embrace AI while staying rooted in their biblical mission. We'd love to continue this journey with you.

Visit ai-for-churches.com to:

- Share your story
- Ask questions
- Join our community
- Schedule a consultation

Together, we can help your church leverage these powerful new tools to expand your impact while maintaining the authentic, personal connections that are at the heart of effective ministry.

www.ingramcontent.com/pod-product-compliance
Lightning Source LLC
LaVergne TN
LVHW021600070426
835507LV00014B/1875